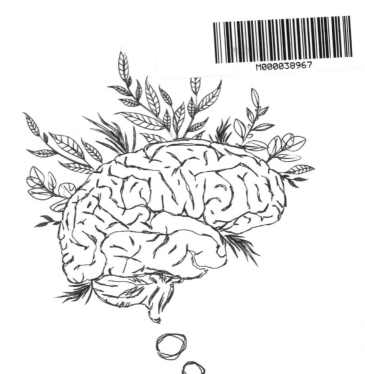

mind captions

samantha hanna

isbn: 978-0-578-39696-5

i can only hope that one day,
i will pick up this book and wonder
what the hell i was thinking.

it would mean that i had the courage
to put something out into the world
and grow from it.

<u>dedication</u>

for every soul,
making its way through life,
calling out for someone to listen,
just to feel heard,
loved,
and understood.

for every soul,
searching for an ounce of hope,
a sense of belonging,
a feeling of inspiration,
an "it's going to be okay".

this book is for you.

let it be your safe place
to sit back,
unwind,
and to reflect
on the deepest parts of you.

both when your heart is glowing,
and when your heart is *breaking*.

cry as you need,
smile when you are compelled to,
but above all,
never stop your heart from feeling,

it's what makes you human.

table of contents

to my readers:

i know this is the section of the book where i was supposed to
put together an organized table of contents for you.

as someone who has spent my whole life
trying to do what *"makes sense"*
i understand that would have been the logical thing to do,
as an author.

writing a table of contents would have helped you understand
what to expect in my collection and may have guided you to a
specific section of the book.

i get it.

but here is the thing:
life is one giant emotional rollercoaster and quite frankly,
nothing about writing this book made any sense when i
started.

i simply began with an idea...
so as you sit (or stand) with this book,
wondering if it is worth the read,
i would like to ask you to come on a journey with me.

let me respectfully take certainty away from you
for the next 136 pages.

though i cannot promise you that every (or any) poem
will resonate with you, i will say that **uncertainty** was the
foundation of this book and one of the greatest gifts i have
ever embraced.

i have put together a collection of thoughts,
in no particular order,

to capture the ever-evolving,
seasons of our lives.

these captions embody:
love, fear, pain, strength, vulnerability, faith,
and so much more...

but just as we do not come with a table of contents on how to
proceed—neither does this book.

so, cheers to the journey of the unpaved road,
and this crazy thing called *life*.

you are earth,
you are water,
you are fire,
you are air,
you are a human in your element
who was created to create.

you are the ocean
calmly dancing along the horizon
while fiercely reminding the earth
just how powerful you are.

[you are the soul of alchemy]

do all things;

make them look easy.
show no fear,
show no pain.

waste the good times
because you're too damn afraid to feel good;
that's too uncertain.

overthink to prepare
just in case your world suddenly comes crashing down,
then crumble all on your own.
but,
that's
okay,
because you've got all you need to numb every ounce of pain
you can't stand to feel,
let alone show.

[sex, money, work, drugs, alcohol, gambling, social media]

anything to distract you from acknowledging the hurt,
anything to keep you from being vulnerable,
anything to keep you from being less than perfect.

and then, just get back up like nothing ever happened,
because if you can give the perception of perfection,
your vices will take care of everything else.

head up,
shoulders back,
façade on,
play it cool.
that's how it's done in this paradox world we live in?

we're all just *"busy and fine"*—and that's not okay.
it's no wonder we've lost touch with each other
when we barely have a grip on reality.

they say some things cannot coexist as one:
{life & death}
{peace & war}
{truths & lies}
{silence & noise}
{light & darkness}
and yet here you are:
{falling apart and recreating yourself}

all at once.

too many people go around
treating others how they are treated.
when they are loved, they love.
when they are hated, they hate.
when they are cheated, they cheat.
when they are ignored, they ignore,
when they are judged, they judge.
they **react** instead of live—
*because they have forgotten how to just **live**.*
that is *weakness.*

i do not consider myself to be particularly artistic—
unless we're talking about my mind overthinking...
then i am a creative fucking genius.

i was never a homebody
until
home became your arms
and
i never wanted to leave...

i may not know the purpose of life,
but i know it's not to fit into this little world.

where perfectly filtered photos
have become perfectly filtered lives;

where connections at our fingertips
make the world seem smaller
and yet minimize our tolerance of one another;

where we settle and survive
conforming to superficial habits
and lose our ability to thrive.

i may not know the purpose of life,
but i know it's not to fit into this little world.

where we drown ourselves in "more"
just to keep up
with everyone around us;

where we stare into screens and cameras
that have become clear glass windows into empty souls,
searching for likes and validation
instead of nurturing all of the love around us;

where we have forgotten how beautiful it is
to simply be ourselves
in a world that is constantly making us someone else;

where the amount of money you have trumps
the amount of good you put in the world.

i may not know the purpose of life,
but i certainly know it's not to fit into this little world.

you are wasting away with each day,
measuring your beauty against some number on a scale,
and suffocating your very being into a shrunken body
where you do not belong,
just to be that girl,
whom society has convinced you,
you must be.

but i must tell you, my dear:
you do not need to keep doing this to yourself.
you do not need to be that girl,
and loving yourself does not need to be an act of rebellion.

you see,
there is so much to love—and that number, those pounds
will never even begin to amount to the beauty that lives inside.

they never wanted an answer;
they didn't need your solutions.
they had heard your advice
from everyone before you.

they just needed you to listen;
and yet you
put that pressure on yourself.

he did not try to tear down the walls she built around her heart;
he made sure she knew they were surrounded by a safe haven

[just in case]

she ever wanted to take a stroll around.

there is nothing wrong with you but
even the most beautiful flowers
will die in a garden surrounded by weeds.

the truth is that it was never about you;
you are fucking magic.

this beautiful, genuine, raw, imperfectly, perfect soul
meant to radiate your energy out into this world, as you are.

so please
stop surrounding yourself with toxic people
who have no right to a heart like yours.

stop
questioning yourself against their words,
judging and analyzing your every move,
and camouflaging just to fit in and feel safe.

stop
apologizing for not being like them,
shrinking yourself to justify their actions,
and measuring your worth based on their validation.

**you are fighting for people who do not care about you and
sure as hell do not deserve you.**

they are not your people and i promise you:
they are not building you up,
if all you ever hear them do is tear others down.

let them go.

i sit here and your words flood my mind:
"they are just words"— you said.
but i cannot accept that.

how can you say "they are just words"
when both their presence and absence have meaning?
they are not just words.

words bring meaning to life,
they bring "life to life"—
each letter strung together,
each word embodying one context or another,
each expression, whether written or spoken,
connects us or separates us from each other.

it's a "human to human" sort of thing, you see.
we either spread love or hate, and that is a choice.

so, to say "they are just words" is to rid them
of meaning and emotion, to undermine their power.

they are not just words.
sometimes less is more; sometimes more is less,
but words always matter.

self-awareness
is a tough pill to swallow
but the medicine your growth so desperately needs.

it's about being unapologetically honest,
taking the time to get in tune with yourself,
and laying out every part of you for you to see:

the good,
the trauma,
your strengths,
your weaknesses,
what lights you up and brings out the best in you,
the little things that drive you crazy,
the gut punches,
and anything that scares you.

once you can do that
you will start to understand
your perceptions of the world and those around you.

**because we do not experience the world as it—
we experience the world as we are.**

it was the scattered molecules
of sunrises and sunsets
that reminded her:
there was ***beauty in chaos.***

mind captions

your problem is that you judge yourself
based on how others treat you.
you try too hard to be "perfect" in everyone's eyes
because you are afraid to lose them.

but the funny part?

you are not afraid to lose them because you need them.
you are afraid to lose them
because you think it is a poor reflection of your character.

so you swallow the blame for their actions,
and you lose yourself instead...

i crave to know the depths of your being;
tell me the tales of your mind
and show me the colors of your heart.
let me see your voice and hear your thoughts.

your vulnerability is the key to mine.

it's easy to give in and be jaded
because love's not exactly panning out the way
you thought it would.

love is not *what* everyone else said it is supposed to be;
love is not *when* everyone else said it is supposed to be.

that is not love, my dear.
that is everyone else's idea of love...

"everyone else" does not get to tell you
what love is supposed to be;
"everyone else" does not get to tell you
when love is supposed to be.

love is like the sunrise and the sunset.
its beauty and magnificence is
in its own timing and its own creation.

so please do not give in and do not be jaded by
everyone else and their "supposed-to-be's";

they tend to fuck good things up.

you carried the mind of a child
and walked through life
as though you were walking along the oceanside.

sifting through sand and collecting treasures of all kinds,
you buried those gems of emotions and experiences
deep within your subconscious mind.

day after day, you held them tight,
but little did you know that
they would try to keep you safe when the time was right.

with the years, life passes you by;
the child's mind you once carried
evolves like the colors of the open sky.

those gems you thought were keeping you safe
are just keeping you small—
fear, anxiety, pain, and trauma embody them all.

they make you someone you never intended to be,
filtering the parts of you that you like
and hiding the ones you do not wish to see.

you hurt deep down,
wondering how this pain in your life ever came to be,
while searching for answers and needing change desperately.

the problem is that you are fighting
an eternal war against your conscious mind,
one battle after the next, you keep fighting,
losing time and time again to your *subconscious mind.*

it's time you empty your sand pail,
sift through the sea glass,
and examine those things you once thought were treasures.

they are weighing you down,
taking up space they do not deserve;

it's time you leave them behind.

mind captions

maybe you didn't run out of things to say.
maybe you just ran out of filtered things to say.

maybe, that's just it...

maybe the things you want to say will shake things up.
maybe they are the exact things that need to be said.

i will stand
for you
when you
cannot stand for yourself.

i will speak
for you
when you
cannot speak for yourself.

i will reflect
the love, strength, and courage
that lives deep within your bones.

time and time again,
i will fight to show you
that you were given a place in this world
and you deserve to be here.

time and time again,
i will fight to show you
that you deserve more than
to just be tolerated.

time and time again,
i will fight to show you
that you deserve to be loved,
as you are and not as someone wants you to be

**because it is the ones who cannot accept themselves that
cannot accept others.**

i came as i was,
you came as you were:
two imperfectly perfect people,
each with our own messy version of life
laid out for the other to see.

you loved me as i was,
i loved you as you were:
two perfectly imperfect messes
never meant to be cleaned up.

...you
are
the
clarity
to
my
C H A O S.

trying to prove your worth
doesn't mean they don't value you.
trying to prove your worth
means you don't value yourself.

both the good and the bad
are living proof of the worlds that reside in you and i.
worlds, i tell you—just waiting and wanting to explode
into the realms of possibility;
possibilities of who we are,
who we can be,
and what we can put into this world.

you see:
humans were created
with the inherent need to create.
it is the ways in which we perceive
and interact with our world that define
the product of that creativity,
both the good and the bad.

our truest potential lies at the heart of this manifestation.

being in a relationship
while constantly trying to change
every little thing
that makes you both who you are
is not love,

it is destruction.

i didn't need a pill.
i didn't need a pep talk.
i just needed someone who would listen,
and the most uncomfortable part about it?

is that anxiety and depression did not tell me
it was my fault for feeling like this,
you did.

i am the leaf falling from its tree
who am i?
where do i belong?
what do i believe?

i am the leaf being blown away by the winds that surround me
should i follow your path?
should i follow their path?
what if i have my own path i'd like to see?

i am the leaf rustling amidst the day and night
what will you think?
what will they think?
will i ever be enough?

i am the leaf torn to pieces by the weight placed on me
how can i be less than perfect?
how can i feel broken?
when each and every sacrifice was meant to build me?

i am the child of immigrant parents you see;
i am the leaf falling from its tree.

i went to the party:

i welcomed discomfort,
with open arms.

i mingled with insecurity,
sharing the stories of our imagination.

i danced with fear,
from one song to the next.

i embraced self-doubt,
with just a kiss.

i laughed at them all,
knowing two could play this game,

and then left with confidence,
knowing that's exactly why i came.

there is a huge part of you
that wants to give up on everything you've ever wanted
because you have failed and you have lost hope.

you don't know how to believe in yourself,
even when you know everything that you *need to do.*
you don't know how to believe in yourself,
even when you have everything that you *need to have.*

i know that place and how disheartening it can be
but deep down, you were not made to play small.

so even as the doubts roar,
listen to the whispers telling you to get back up.

you are better than this
and now is not the time to give up on yourself.

find your way again.

the friends you need to keep in your life are not:
the ones who make you someone you are not,
the ones who make you prove your worth,
the ones who constantly make you question their intentions,
or the ones who need excuses for their actions.
the friends you need to keep in your life?

[these people]
they are not perfect, but they are the ones who:
will go through hell with you,
make you laugh *to a point of no return,*
and teach you how to be vulnerable.

[these people]
are the ones who don't need the explanations,
they will tell you when *they* are wrong
but more importantly, when *you* are too.

[these people]
are the ones who
remind you that life was
never meant to be done
alone.

keep them close.

you threw your words around
like they could not hurt anyone.
time and time again, you threw them—
but the harder you threw them,
the faster they came back around
to knock you down like a
boomerang.

what is holding you back
is not your fear of failure.

you're scared of your potential,
you're scared to succeed;
because to succeed,
is to stand up to the demons that tell you you're not enough.

but you were made with a backbone much stronger than you
know—*pick your head up and straighten it out, sis.*

if you want to rise,
you must walk your way to the top.
but if you want to be respected,
you cannot tiptoe.

"<u>the morning of</u>"

i type a few words.
i check my phone.
i sip my coffee.
i check my phone.
i take a few glances, speak to a few people.
i check my phone.
looking for a sign—
wanting and hoping so badly that there will be a reason.
because a reason will let me hold on to what i had hoped will
happen.

hour by hour,
the day goes by.
hour by hour,
i check my phone.
nothing.

you said you'd call—
and yet here i sit with nothing at all.
not. a. single. damn. thing.

until i realized that "nothing" was everything i needed.
"nothing" was my sign.

i had to let go of what i had hoped would happen
for a taste of what was actually happening.

"nothing" was my chance
to choose myself for the first time.

i wasn't going to call you
because "maybe something happened"
or "maybe i misunderstood you".
i had swallowed the blame and given you the benefit of the
doubt before,
but even hope expires sometimes.

…this was that time.

let me tell you something:
i already know too much.

i know about your passion,
even though you try to hide it sometimes.
i know about your big dreams and
where you would like them to take you.

i know about the jump you need to make
in order to get yourself there.

i know it's a scary one,
and that's exactly why you keep holding yourself back.

but let me tell you something else, my dear:

whether or not you would like to believe it,
you have everything you could possibly ever need.

yes, your life is going to continue to unravel
and many things will change,
but at some point, you will realize that you will never be able
to put out that fire of yours.

you are going to need to hold on tightly
to each and every one of those fears
and take the leap of faith,
knowing wholeheartedly that you will fall and it will hurt.

but you know what?

you will gather up enough courage to make that jump,
you will find success somewhere on the other side,
and those cuts and bruises?

***they will just be proof of the strength
you've been given to rise.***

if
you
were
not
pretending
to
be
someone

[for everyone else]

...who would you be?

it's happened so many times before
that you've learned to push people away,
and when they do happen to make their way inside,
you just sit back and wait for them to screw you over,
because you've lost your faith in knowing
that good people still exist.

i get it.

but please, do not let this world harden you and steal your
goodness.

you're screwing yourself over.

what is funny to me is [*not*]:
        that one day we feel unstoppable
        and the next, we are drowning in our sorrows;

what is funny to me is [*not*]:
        that we meet new people,
        travel to new places, and fall in love—
        while simultaneously losing the people we cannot
        live without and facing the biggest disappointments
        from those we thought would never hurt us;

what is funny to me is [*not*]:
        that we can stare back in awe,
        at the person we have grown to be—
        then
        lose the job,
        lose the friends,
        lose the opportunities,
        lose the hope;

what is funny to me is [*not*]
        that we have control over many things,
        yet our emotions have a life of their own;

what is funny to me is:
        that we somehow think we need to have
        this crazy life all figured out.

the thing is,
we're all human;
we fuck up in more ways than we can imagine.
we hurt the ones we love
and love the ones who hurt us.
we do it all the time—
sometimes intentionally
and sometimes unintentionally.
we are not right or wrong, just imperfect.

you cannot take what you cannot control personally.
you cannot let the actions
or inactions of others disturb your inner peace.
it's not fair to you or them.

because the thing is,
we're all human
and we fuck up in more ways
than we can imagine.

i do not speak to be heard;
i speak to be voiced.

why am i sitting here asking you for permission to heal?

it is not selfish to need time
to unravel the parts of me that are hurting.

it is not selfish to need space
to prioritize my well-being, inner peace, and happiness.

it is not selfish to need empathy
to learn how to love myself again.

if you cannot understand that
then not parting ways
—would be selfish of us both.

you are beautiful
[*but lose some of that weight of yours*]

you are beautiful
[*but cover up with some of that makeup of yours*]

you are beautiful
[*but put on more of that smile of yours*]

you are beautiful
[*but soften up that hardened soul of yours*]

you are beautiful
[*but remember that sensitivity is a weakness of yours*]

you are beautiful
[*but watch that voice of yours*]

you are beautiful
[*but confine those dreams of yours*]

you are beautiful
[*but fit into this box of OURS*]

sincerely,
[*s o c i e t y*]

breathe:
take it all in;
let your lungs fill with every ounce of air.

think:
but not for too long;
let your mind wander without a care.

feel:
for you are human after all;
let your heart sing its song and tell its share.

i write because there are so many things
that i wish i could tell my younger self:

doing what you are told
does not make you good or bad.

doing what you are told makes you obedient
but
there are some times in life
when you will need to say "no".

say "no" to the things in your life
that drain you of your energy
and have nothing to show for it.

say "no" to shitty cups of coffee,
plans you never wanted,
and people who never wanted you.

say "no" to negativity, the distractions,
and anything you cannot love with your entire heart.

if it is the worst thing you do,
you will be quite alright.

you are not lost
and you are not stuck;
you are just sitting at a crossroads
between
where you have been,
where you are,
where you're supposed to go,
and where you want to go.

you have all you need to get you there,
but here you sit,
trapped by resistance
and overwhelmed with frustration
because you know your potential.

here you sit,
trying to protect yourself
from both the "wrong" and "right" ways.

you are not lost
and you are not stuck;
you are just sitting at a crossroads
and need to know:

life is not about answers.
there is no map
and there is no "right" way;
there is only a conscious choice
to either move towards the unknown or not.

because no matter where the unknown leads,
it is infinitely more rewarding than
sitting at a crossroads,
mentally exhausting yourself to nowhere.

they hurt you,
but resenting them
will only give that hurt
a permanent place to reside.

maybe i did not want to learn my lessons;
maybe you were the one person who,
no matter how many times i pushed away,
i secretly hoped you'd always come back....

there is something so fucking beautiful
about being at peace with yourself
and understanding that your growth needs no audience.

samantha hanna

how incredibly euphoric it is
to lie my body down
with the weight of my stress,
sinking to the very edges of my body.

my lungs inhale
and my belly fills up with air,
soaking up every bit
of calmness and peace i can.

my lungs exhale
and my body becomes weightless,
releasing every ounce of pain and suffering.

my mind is brought to a moment
of pure stillness amidst the chaos,
where i can hear nothing and everything.

how beautiful it is to be
here and now,
even for just a moment.

there will be many times in your life when you'll be told:
who you need to be,
what you need to do,
and how you need to do it.
but
there is something so incredibly beautiful
about making a decision to start silencing the noise of the
world around you so that you can start to
listen to the voices inside you.

it's about showing up for yourself and giving yourself the
love, support, and compassion you desperately need.

it's about healing.

it's about doing what's truly best for you and letting go of
anyone and anything that gets in the way of your happiness.

it's about leaning into both fear and excitement,
making a conscious effort to intentionally find whatever it is
that sets your soul on fire,
and going after it with your whole heart.

none of us are perfect,
but your superpower isn't in being perfect.

it's in being vulnerable,
being authentic,
and being human—
because if you can do that,
then you can show others that
they can too.

there was nothing particularly special
about how she looked—
her hair loosely held back
in a wild mess of a bun,
her face naturally illuminating a beauty
that no make-up could ever compete with,
her body clothed in the freedom
of an oversized sweater
and a pair of stretched out leggings.

to most, it was nothing particularly special,
and yet, she looked in the mirror,
smiling with a sense of sweet defiance
towards everything she had been taught about beauty.
that alone made it special.

you struggle to let people in
and to show them *your* version of life,
because
at the end of the day,
it's easier to just put a smile on.

emotions are too messy.

[us] humans have this distorted idea of perfection.
we chase it as if we are chasing our own shadow.
each time we get closer, it escapes out grasp.
quit chasing something you already are.

mind captions

somewhere in your mind,
you crammed me into a little box,
full of assumptions,
with some sort of label for all to see,
instead of admitting that you may not know
all there is to know about me.
because to do otherwise,
would be an act of defiance
and it was just easier to judge me instead.

well, i'm sure glad one of us is comfortable.

i hope you give yourself the chance to feel, the chance to heal, the chance to be the person you've always needed.

i hope you recognize all that you have to offer and give yourself the chance to be less than perfect—
yet, more than enough.

i hope you stop trying to do what "makes sense" just to keep yourself safe, at the expense of what truly brings you happiness.

i hope you stand as you are and cultivate an environment that gives you the chance to grow.

i hope you cherish the love around you, knowing you deserve every ounce of it and pour it right back into everything you do.

i hope you intentionally lean into fear and excitement, trust yourself along the way, and give yourself the chance to fail in order to shine.

i hope you know you're exactly what this world needs and when you can find your own light, you can pass it along and help others do the same.

it hurt to let you go,
but it hurt even more
not knowing what would come next...

[*i wanted answers that were not there*]

and so i allowed myself to sit
in the discomfort of uncertainty
with nothing to fill the void or mask the pain,
knowing one thing for sure...

[*i had time on my side*]

time would give me space.
time would give me clarity.
time would give me opportunity.

[*to get in tune with who i was before you*]

to strive to become a better version of myself;
to solidify what i wanted,
what needed,
and what i deserved.

maybe life would bring us back together
or maybe it would keep us apart...

[*but that was not for me to figure out right now*]

right now, i needed to tend to my own happiness
more than anything else that would try
to get in between
it and i.

[*time would give me answers*]

you are not there yet
because you are not supposed to be there—
or maybe it's because you were never
supposed to be there in the first place?

[expectations will do that to a person]

i have found that
one of life's most difficult lessons
is learning how to give a fuck
about the things in life that truly matter
and letting go of everything else.

[what a balancing act it is]

you come and go
like the tides of the ocean,
and here i sit at the edge,
just waiting to be kissed.

to the little girl inside me
who just wanted to be told
"you're just as beautiful as the other girls":
i think about you often,
reminiscing about the days when
i walked in your shoes and lived in your skin.
some days, those days don't seem so far away.

it's funny how emotions never leave a person.
you just wanted to fit in, to be like the pretty girls.
so, you fought and fought to change
the most beautiful part about you:
your differences.

you didn't know it then,
but you were fighting an uphill battle—
and an unwinnable one at that.

i wish i could tell you then
that you were *not* the problem
and change was the easy part.
i wish i could tell you then
that you'd never be able to brush
self-hate under the rug.
i wish i could tell you
that it was all an illusion:
this idea of "perfection"
that you were striving for...

maybe it would have saved you
from the tears and the heartache
and from being so damn hard on yourself.

i wish i could tell you
that you are never going to be happy
trying to look and be like everyone else.
i wish i could tell you
that God did not waste your potential
and neither should you.

all i can do is pass it along
to the little girl today who is
someone else's daughter
and just wants to be told:
"you're just as beautiful as the other girls."
the one who feels uncomfortable in her own skin,
the one who hates looking in the mirror
because she's been taught to hate what she sees,
the one who thinks she will be able to love herself
if she just loses a few pounds or looks like someone else,
the one who wants nothing more than to change
and constantly wonders whether she will ever be enough.

i see you, i feel you, i have been in your shoes,
and i still walk in your footprints.

let me tell you everything
i wish i could have told myself:
you are more than a body
and the lies you have been told
to believe about yourself.
you are exactly what this world needs.
more than beautiful,
less than perfect,
and always enough.
you're the warrior.
thanks for being my hero.

i want you to remember one thing:
you don't need to do what everyone else is doing.
take your time to figure out who you want to be
and what kind of life you want to lead.
keep whatever it is that makes you happy
and brings peace—closest to you.

your sanity may look like someone else's insanity,
and that is ***more than okay.***

she is a wild rose.

strong yet delicate,
her roots run deep,
holding on and weathering every storm
that tries to break her down.

day after day,
she blossoms into
the wild rose she is.

12:48 a.m.
my head weighs down on my pillow,
my body glides against my silk sheets as i
toss
and
turn
minute after minute,
my ears hear nothing but the sound
of my fingertips tapping on my mattress,
my eyes open and close but want nothing
more than to slip into a deep dream,
my mind races, thinking about everything
and seemingly nothing at all.
on
and
on
my mind races, thinking about everything
and seemingly nothing at all.
my eyes open and close but want nothing
more than to slip into a deep dream,
my ears hear nothing but the sound
of my fingertips tapping on my mattress,
my body glides against my silk sheets as i
toss
and
turn
minute after minute,
my head weighs down on my pillow,

insomnia lets the hours go by,
but *reality* reminds me it's only
12:49 a.m.

i just couldn't understand
why things didn't work out...
i blamed myself—
trying to change this and that.
until i realized that i could've changed
everything about myself
and things still would've never worked out.

because "me" was not who you were looking for,
and i could not be *her*.
so, here i will stand as myself
and let you love her instead...

i looked each and every last insecurity
dead in the face and felt **nothing**.
somehow—this was *freedom*.

perfection looked at me and said:
"i'm sorry for all of the struggles you have faced
for which i cannot relate to."

i
inhaled
deeply
and
with
my
exhale

i could not help but smile and say:
"i'm sorry for all of the struggles you haven't faced,
for my struggles are what have built me."

mind captions

i have not lived through your tragedies
just as you have not lived through mine,
but together, we share a collection of tragedies
that could make the whole world cry;

your struggles are as real to you
as mine are real to me—
and yet, we push each other away
as if "we are so different"...
why?

please do not allow yourself to water it down,
to
forget
what
real
love
is
just to avoid the hurt of moving on.
i know settling feels better right now,
but you deserve much more than settling, my dear.
you
deserve
real
love.

it was a series of highs and lows,
which oscillated in a way
that somehow balanced out
and almost felt normal.

it was as if the highs weren't enough to push me,
but the lows weren't enough to push me either.

and there i sat
[in the awkward middle]
with no real reason to change at all...

with courage
(*the heart stuff*)
comes clarity
(*the mind stuff*)

just as puzzles
are not sold in single pieces,
this is me;
take me as a whole or not at all.

samantha hanna

some of the things you complain about
are the same things someone else is praying for.
so while you are praying to be in someone else's shoes,
someone is praying for shoes.

i crave simplicity in the complex,
beauty in the struggle,
and rawness.

i crave vulnerability in the utmost way,
strength in softness,
and imperfection.

it is not our differences that jeopardize humanity;
it is a loss of empathy towards ourselves and one another.

we are being taught to simply *survive*
in a world that continues to threaten our authenticity
by telling us who we need to be in order to be loved.

we are being raised to believe that
we *must fit in* & *be perfect*
in order to be *accepted*,
so we spend our whole lives hating ourselves
to serve the interests of a few.

and how can we accept others
if we have not learned how to accept ourselves?

you see,
it is a loss of empathy towards
ourselves and one another,
not
our
differences—*that jeopardize humanity.*

it was a vivid blur:
a moment of wild spontaneity
a kiss of both strength and softness,
something i could not fully explain.

it was a feeling of euphoria
that reminded me what it was like
to believe in magic.
it was what i call
a heartbeat kiss.

samantha hanna

they
cannot
burn
a
soul
that *is already on fire.*

i know you feel broken,
but please know that is okay.
do not try to put yourself back
together in the same way.

have you ever seen a mosaic?
so many pieces once shattered as can be—
and yet, back together, they come.
that is the essence of beauty.

you are not naive.
in fact, you are so far from it.
you just want so badly
to find the innocent goodness
your own heart carries
in everyone you meet.

she could not stop the anxiety
that flooded her mind and body
but
    day
 by
    day
she
    learned
how
    to

ride the waves.

one day,
i just realized
what little fun came in *settling* for perfection.

my dear,
until you know and accept
the fact that you are deserving of love,
you will never be capable of receiving it.

understand this:
there will always be
people, places, and things
that try to pull you back
as you try your hardest to grow.

old habits, old relationships, and old thoughts
will creep their way back into your life—
time and time again.
but much like before,
they are not meant to stay.
they are simply there
to see if you've learned your lessons.
s a y *h e l l o...*

...s a y *g o o d b y e.*

mind captions

sometimes it's like my mind is
at war against itself,
fighting to justify you and your actions
while trying to run far, far away
from anything to do with you.

and here i sit,
in the middle of this
heart tug-of-war.

the ones who are the most insecure
and afraid of being judged
are the ones who judge
because
putting you in the spotlight,
keeps them out of it.

one of the most beautiful things about life
is that it's made up of a series of subtleties—
days that, when put together, become months
and months that become years—
years of both the best and worst times of our lives.

at the end of the day, just remember to
make those subtleties add up to
something great,
something "not so subtle".

i put up walls
to keep myself safe,
but deep down:

i
secretly
want
you
to
break
them

to let the floodgates open,
and for me to feel safe drowning in your heart.

you sat back and laughed at me
like i was the crazy one.
you lied to me over and over,
telling me i was not enough;
telling me i needed more people, more things,
more achievements, more validation
to fill the voids—
and somehow, when you spoke,
i was the first one to sit and listen.

you took so much of my time to watch me suffer
because you could not stand to see me happy,
but your only power was the power i gave you.

and that's when i woke up and said:
fuck you, depression.

it's not over.
i know you feel otherwise:
like you've come this far
and maybe this is it...
maybe this is all you've got and this is as far as you were
meant to go...

these are your limits
and here is your finish line.
maybe it is, but what if it's not?
what if there is so much more out there for you?
what if you haven't even scratched the surface of your
potential?
did you ever think that maybe it's just a matter of getting
unstuck?

it happens to the very best of us, my dear:
we fall,
we rise,
we break,
and we mold ourselves a little more each day.

you see,
you are allowed to feel the way you are feeling.
and even though you may not see it or understand it now:
it. is. necessary.

the time you think you are wasting each time you fail
is everything but wasted.
it is teaching you how to love,
not only the journey but yourself.
it is teaching you how to love yourself—with each and every
one of your flaws.

do not let that fire of yours get washed away
by the tears you cry.
you are right where you need to be,
so let these tears be the gasoline to your fire,
which has just begun...

mind captions

do not tell me "it will be okay"
as i sit here and shatter.
do not tell me the things
you think i want to hear.

time will pass, but this?
this will not subside.
so hug me tightly,
but please save us both and say
nothing at all.

if you are always worried
about being for them,
you will never know
the beauty that exists
in being for *you*.

mind captions

i had an empty canvas,
clear as the open sky.
i had a set of paint brushes,
full of colored dye:
one red—dipped in fear,
one blue—submerged in failure,
one gray—saturated in uncertainty,
one yellow—soaked in hope,
and there i sat with the audacity to paint;
every dream of mine,
one stroke at a time.

your words are the sugar in my tea,
not because they are *sweet*
and what i *want* to hear
but because they are **raw**
and what i **need** to hear.

sometimes, i catch myself
slipping into a daydream,
wondering what our love would be like.

i catch myself
when all i want to do
is keep on slipping...

i feel anxious
because nothing is happening
when i thought it would
or *how i thought it would.*
and as the days pass,
the anxiety sets in deeper,
telling me "i am not enough".

some days, i think myself into a panic attack.
some days, i think myself into a depression.
some days, i mentally spiral out of control.

i try to piece everything together
and make it happen,
because that gives me a false sense of control
when i can't see an answer or the light
at the end of the tunnel.

let me just say:
that never works.

and it hurts even more
because now, i am trying
and it is still not working.
so, maybe trying isn't what i need.
maybe there is a space between
doing what i know with what i have
and *not doing anything with what i do not know,*
living on the edge and letting serendipity do its thing.

rejection
is what you needed.
because rejection
taught you how to choose *yourself.*

we have been taught to hide
and we have been taught to take on life alone,
because to survive on our own
"must be" a sign of strength.

but is it, really?

we were born with the inherent gift to love and empathize.
so, to carry on alone is to rid ourselves of these very gifts.

for it is through
vulnerability that we connect,
empathy that we thrive,
and love that we rise.

[*this is strength*]

if i cannot love you without thought,
then i cannot love you at all.

i think the most inspiring people are:
the ones who show their struggle,
the ones who aren't living the picture-perfect life,
the ones who are brave enough to shake things up,
the ones going after their dreams—
knowing wholeheartedly that
there is no straight path to them,
the ones who know that they will fall flat on their face
from time to time and yet, despite this, they continue to step
one
foot
in
front
of the other.

carrying a bruised up heart, a tired soul
and wanting nothing more than to persist
in the midst of their struggle,
they.
step.
onward.

perfectionism is a fearful façade of the ego,
a poison to the authentic,
and a voice constantly screaming
"i am not enough".

i knew you were genuine
because genuine is all i felt
i needed to be around you.

you are lonely because you have learned
that it's better to sit in silence
than to be bombarded by static noise.

the way you challenge me
like no one else can
is what i love and hate
about you most.

love
does not
fail;
people fail.

it's not him,
it's not you;
it's the way you're approaching it all.

there is nothing wrong with you
wanting to feel loved,
but there is something wrong with you
thinking that you need to constantly fight for his attention.

dropping subtle hints,
and hoping that one day,
you will be enough.

he sees right through you
and it makes him try less.

because why should he try
when you already try so hard?

you had his attention
until you started fighting for it.

he wanted to get to know you
when you were not trying
to get him to want to know you.

so, put yourself out there.
but for love's sake,
stop trying so hard.

be still,
be vulnerable,
and live in the temporary uncertainty
of not knowing whether he will like you back.
because if he does, you will know it.
and it will be *you* that he wants to get to know,
not the girl desperately fighting for his love and attention.

i know you want to tell me you are "okay"
because that is easy.
but i know you are struggling
because i know what it is to struggle.

and while i don't know your struggle,
i don't need to know it
for you to know that i am here.

i am here.

those words alone.
to tell me more or tell me less,
that is up to you—
but please know that i am here.

"a life jacket called bullshit"

i outgrew the old me a long time ago—
the people,
the habits,
the mentality,
the negativity.

i know that i want more than anything to change,
but i have been holding on to "the old" for dear life.

i know that i want more than anything to change,
but i am scared to let go and to give up the gift of certainty.

i know that i want more than anything to change, but all i am
doing is treading water in a life jacket called bullshit.

i outgrew the old me a long time ago.
so, what the hell am i doing?

change is scary,
but lack of it is terrifying.

change is scary,
*but i don't want to be this person, knowing that i was made for
so much more than this.*

change is scary,
but the bitterness and regret are killing me.

change is scary,
but i can't take it and i won't take it.

change is scary,
*but the longer i tread water, the sooner i drown in an ocean
where i was meant to swim.*

your feeling of entitlement
is **not** my consent.
this is still *my* body.

i knew
i had lost myself
when i had surpassed
every one of your expectations,
but had never felt like more of a failure.

i know you are only trying
to keep your little girls safe
from the harshness of this world.

you cannot stand to see
our hearts break,
so you protect us
from every ounce of pain
you possibly can.

i know you are only trying
to keep your little girls safe
from the tears of this world.

you cannot see our minds struggle,
so you protect us
from every ounce of worry
you possibly can.

and with each day you build us up,
i cannot help but wonder
how you still stand so tall
through the pain,
through the tears,
through the worries,
that would have made most crumble.

you wear the wounds
and lock up the pain
as if they never happened.
you stand so tall,
just to keep us safe,
just to see us smile.

there is no bigger waste of potential
than a soul that's
too scared to try,
too scared to fail.

because "too scared to try, too scared to fail"
is the biggest failure of them all.

i do not like to think much when i write;
thinking ruins masterpieces.

i think there is something
to be said about humans
always wanting what we don't have.

maybe it's not about having anything at all;
but the pursuit of getting it—that keeps us wanting
everything we don't have.

we love the chase.

the truth is that you try too hard.
you try too hard because
your heart is full of so much love
and you just want to find the right people
to pour that love into.

you want to feel loved,
but instead of searching for those people,
maybe you just need to recognize
the ones right in front of you
who would do anything for you.

why do you take them for granted?
is it because you didn't work for their love?
or is it because you feel so undeserving of it?

you would rather chase people
and love those who do not love you,
because they can let you down
and remind you of what you truly feel:
undeserving of love.

sometimes, i just want an answer.
i want to know where this is all going—*if anywhere.*

because waiting is hard
and vulnerability is even harder.

"no" is easier than "maybe"
for my heart to handle.

mind captions

it was as if you came out of nowhere
and gently ripped my heart out of my chest,
only to place it in yours and give it a place to rest.

samantha hanna

we like to pretend that we are all so different,
but many of us are fighting for our lives—
each seeing life through a different lens
and each with a different mountain to climb.

we are all looking for a little hope,
a reason, a sign
to keep fighting for our lives,
even though we like to pretend that we are all so different.

to the girl who knows who and what she wants:
hold strong.

i know you haven't found either yet,
but most people don't even know what they want.

give yourself time, give yourself space.
you are growing,
and if time has taught you anything, it's *who you are—*
and when things don't go as planned,
your character is what shines most.

to the girl who knows
who and what she wants,
yet
questions if it's worth the wait:
hold strong.

it is worth the wait;
you are worth the wait.

some days,
i wish i could sit down
and sip a cup of tea
with my four-year-old self—
to chat for a while and learn a thing or two about life:
like what it's like to live in the moment without expectations,
to dream and to love without limits,
to feel everything so deeply,
to believe in oneself and the goodness of this world,
to embrace gratitude and uncertainty,
and to stand as we are,
long before the world told us who to be.

i know it's eating you up inside—
to feel misunderstood—
but sometimes,
you must be okay with people
not knowing your side of the story.

you know who you are.
now let that shit go.

there is nothing more beautiful than
a perfectly, imperfect,
chaotic mess of a human
in their element.

to live your truth
is to exist in a world
without permission.

because truth does not require validation
and neither should you.

i stand in front of you

i see my reflection in your eyes,
the tides of the ocean running down my face.

i taste the salt of the waters i am drowning in,
i feel the current moving around me.

i stand still
while my world is spinning,
my bones are shivering,
and my heart is breaking over the loss of you.

understand this:
friction is necessary;
it means we are living with the freedom to speak our minds
and to live our truths, though we may not always agree.

friction is necessary;
it reminds us that
each and every one of us has our own version of life
and we see things,
hear things,
feel things,
through our own filters.

friction is necessary;
it reminds us how to look at the world and remember how to
shake things up a bit.

"finding your person" is about finding the person
with whom you have the space to be vulnerable.
it's about showing up as *you*—as you can possibly be.
it's about putting your heart on the line
and giving it the freedom to beat to its own rhythm.
it's about letting that rhythm be a direct extension
of your soul and that which sets it on fire.

"finding your person" is not about changing
who you are at your core or what you believe in.
it's not about altering your rhythm to mimic another's song.
"finding your person" is about fusing your rhythms together
and dancing to the magic of it all.
that is soul music.

mind captions

if
  my
    body
      ran
        as
          much
            as
              my
                mind,
                  there might not be anything left of me.

you will never be enough for some.

when you plant a beautiful flower,
they will tell you about their garden

some people just like to compete;
go flourish instead.

you were like a bottle of honey whiskey:
a sweet defiance that always left me hungover.

i hope you do not wait, my dear.
i hope you choose to live above your fears.
i hope you see your beauty long before someone else.

i hope you rise no matter how many times you fall.
i hope you have the courage to believe in yourself and stand tall.
i hope you learn to embrace your perfect imperfections with each day.

i hope you find wholeness on your own.
i hope you remember that you are never alone.
i hope you speak up because you deserve to be heard too.

i just hope.

it hurt to lose you,
but it hurt even more to still have you there.

on my mind.
in all that the things that i did,
in all the places that i went,
you were there.

conversations
and
moments replayed in my head
and
yet, as much as it hurt,
somehow, i knew...

none of this was enough to have kept you in my life,
and only time could teach me that.

time.

you have always been good enough;
that was never a question.
but realize this:
too often, we self-sabotage to avoid failure.
and in avoiding failure, we miss out on so much success
that we fail by default.

so, the next time you are tempted to avoid the hard things:
vulnerability, uncertainty, judgement, fear, and discomfort,
remember that you are just avoiding success.

i saw a picture of you
smiling
for
the
world
to
see
but deep down i could not help but wonder
were
you
truly
happy?

i could see
the hours on the clock moving,
the colors of the leaves changing.

i could hear
the tides of the ocean crashing,
the sounds of the birds singing.

i could feel
the world around me turning
people, places, and life moving and evolving.

everything changing
while i just sit here
letting my heart crumble, thinking about *you*.

confidence is a commitment
to stand your ground in who you are:
this perfectly, imperfect person
who has strengths and weaknesses
that are constantly evolving as you open yourself up
to learn from the world around you.

confidence is a decision
to neither shrink nor inflate yourself
into the one you "need to be".

it is believing in the evolution of yourself
as you continue to grow into your potential
and empowering others to do the same.

confidence is the flower
that grows in the dark,
through the concrete,
on no timing but its own.

samantha hanna

like the morning sunrise,
like the autumn foliage,
like the calm before the storm,
or the rainbow that follows,

like the evening sunset,
like the moon peeking through the night,
like the caterpillar evolving,
or the butterfly that follows

you are not behind or ahead;
you're exactly where you need to be.

proceed with confidence,
embracing the notion that some of the most
transcendent moments in life
are never planned.

on that day, she saw someone—
an unfamiliar soul whom she had never seen before.
at least, that was her first impression...
it was an unusual feeling and one that perplexed her in every
way.

she stared closely and inquisitively,
taking in every part of the individual's profile.
her eyes slowly traced along the outline
of the body that stood before her.

she examined its features:
the long, dark hair that fell gently
across the shoulders and down the back.
the pale, fragile skin and the dark circles
beneath the eyes that spoke of a tiring journey—
she could see it all.
the more she focused,
the more she could see.

in that very moment and with every ounce of courage,
she allowed her eyes to drift
and meet with the eyes of the person
who so eagerly stared back.

suddenly, everything stopped.

she had never felt so present;
it was as if time had simply disappeared.
as she gazed into the eyes before her,
she saw something she had never seen before:
the eyes were clear, glass windows that illuminated a bright
light of the soul
which was but a few steps away...

however, it was not just any soul.
it was one that had many stories to tell,
but very few had heard.

it spoke of struggles, doubt, times of uncertainty, and of pure
defeat.

it spoke of inner turmoil and everything but peace.

and yet, despite all of this, it was what she saw
even deeper within that soul that left her without words...
as her eyes continued to pierce those in front of her,
she could see an array of vibrant colors dancing inside:
she saw a fire running deep within the veins.
spark by spark, flame by flame, it raged
unlike anything she had ever known.

through the eyes and through that fire,
she saw strength and she saw passion.
she saw a fighter who had fought
more battles than anyone had ever known.
she saw a confident leader and creative genius,
who despite their abilities, knew nothing of the sort.
she saw someone who she simply could not explain.
there were no words, no expressions that could capture
the image that quickly became embedded in her mind.

in what seemed like an everlasting moment of time,
she contemplated everything she had seen.
her mind raced and shuffled as she looked for answers
and tried to put the pieces together.

suddenly, it clicked and all that she felt
could no longer be hidden;
because it came streaming down her face,
tear by tear, as she realized:
she was her.